DIGGING UP THE PAST

DINOSAURS

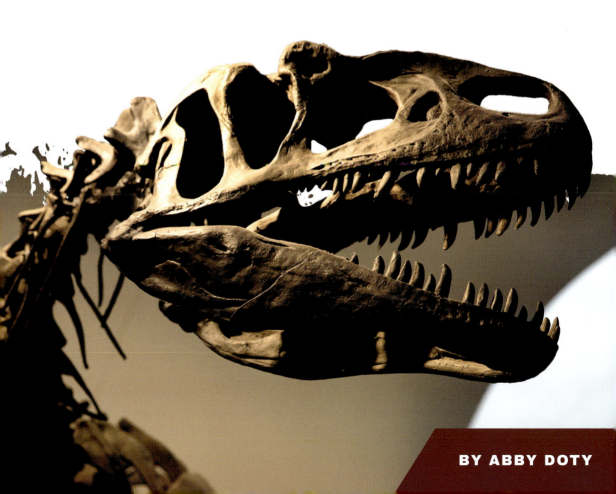

BY ABBY DOTY

WWW.APEXEDITIONS.COM

Copyright © 2026 by Apex Editions, Mendota Heights, MN 55120. All rights reserved. No part of this book may be reproduced or utilized in any form or by any means without written permission from the publisher.

Apex is distributed by North Star Editions:
sales@northstareditions.com | 888-417-0195

Produced for Apex by Red Line Editorial.

Photographs ©: Shutterstock Images, cover, 1, 7, 12, 14–15, 16–17, 21, 24–25, 26; Wellcome Images, 4–5; Mary Morland/Oxford University Museum of Natural History, 6, 29; Arthur Dorety/Stocktrek Images, Inc./Alamy, 8–9; Gideon Mantell/Royal Society of London, 10–11; iStockphoto, 13; Jon G. Fuller/VWPics/AP Images, 18; Alexander Koerner/Getty Images News/Getty Images, 19; Jon Austria/The Daily Times/AP Images, 20; Larry Mayer/The Billings Gazette/AP Images, 22–23; James St. John/Flickr, 27

Library of Congress Control Number: 2025930921

ISBN
979-8-89250-531-4 (hardcover)
979-8-89250-567-3 (paperback)
979-8-89250-637-3 (ebook pdf)
979-8-89250-603-8 (hosted ebook)

Printed in the United States of America
Mankato, MN
082025

NOTE TO PARENTS AND EDUCATORS

Apex books are designed to build literacy skills in striving readers. Exciting, high-interest content attracts and holds readers' attention. The text is carefully leveled to allow students to achieve success quickly. Additional features, such as bolded glossary words for difficult terms, help build comprehension.

TABLE OF CONTENTS

CHAPTER 1
FIRST DINOSAUR 4

CHAPTER 2
FIRST FOSSILS 10

CHAPTER 3
DIGGING UP FOSSILS 16

CHAPTER 4
DINOSAUR DISCOVERIES 22

COMPREHENSION QUESTIONS • 28
GLOSSARY • 30
TO LEARN MORE • 31
ABOUT THE AUTHOR • 31
INDEX • 32

CHAPTER 1

First Dinosaur

In the early 1800s, Professor William Buckland gathered **fossils**. He had several parts of a giant animal's teeth, legs, and spine.

William Buckland collected fossils for many years. Most came from mines in Stonesfield, England.

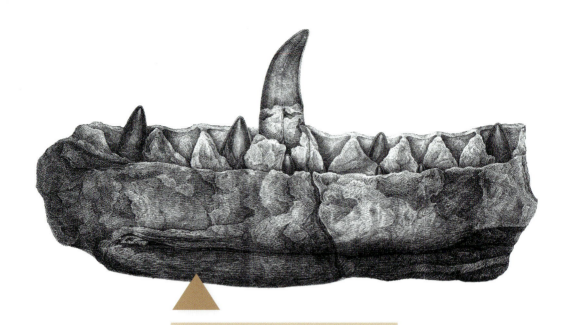

One fossil was a jawbone. Its teeth looked similar to lizard teeth.

In 1824, Buckland showed the fossils to a group of scientists. He said the bones came from a giant lizard. He said this lizard lived long ago. It was more than 40 feet (12 m) long. And it walked on four legs.

BETTER GUESSES

Buckland guessed what the lizard looked like. But he got a few things wrong. Scientists today think it was 30 feet (9 m) long. And it walked on two legs.

In the mid-1800s, people made models of what they thought Buckland's lizard looked like.

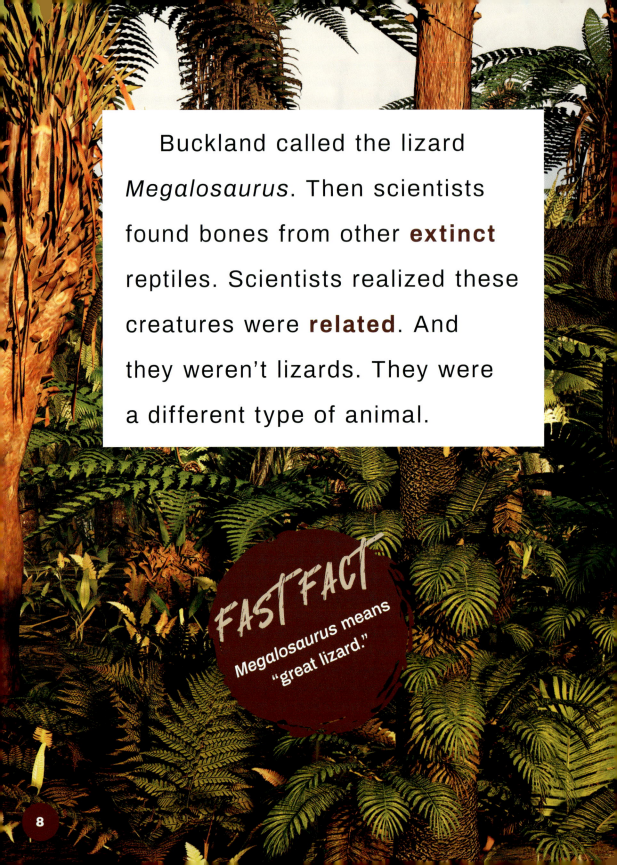

Buckland called the lizard *Megalosaurus*. Then scientists found bones from other **extinct** reptiles. Scientists realized these creatures were **related**. And they weren't lizards. They were a different type of animal.

FAST FACT

Megalosaurus means "great lizard."

Scientists later realized that *Megalosaurus* was a type of dinosaur.

CHAPTER 2

First Fossils

Humans have been finding dinosaur fossils for hundreds of years. These fossils included teeth and bones. At first, people didn't know what animals they belonged to.

In 1822, scientists found fossils of teeth. People later learned they came from a dinosaur called *Iguanodon*.

In the 1800s, scientists found many fossils in England. All looked like bones from large lizards. Scientists called these creatures *dinosaurs*.

Scientists create models of dinosaurs. They guess what each one looked like based on fossils.

Hylaeosaurus was one of the first dinosaurs that people identified.

FAST FACT

Scientists first used the term *dinosaur* in the early 1840s. It means "terrible lizard."

Scientists have identified thousands of different types of dinosaurs.

Scientists found more fossils around the world. They realized that many kinds of dinosaurs had existed. Some were massive. Others were small and quick. Some could swim or fly.

FORMING FOSSILS

Often, fossils form after **sediment** covers dead animals. Soft parts of the animals wear away. But hard parts turn into rock. This change can take millions of years.

CHAPTER 3

Digging Up Fossils

Scientists search for dinosaur fossils in the ground. They use **chisels** to break rocks. Then they brush away dirt and sand.

Scientists search for fossils in areas with lots of rock made from sediment.

Fossils can be fragile. So, scientists handle them carefully. They place the fossils in hard cases. Or they make casts to protect them.

To make casts, scientists cover fossils in strips of cloth and plaster. The casts dry and become hard.

Trace fossils show tracks or signs of ancient life. Footprints are one example.

FAST FACT
Some fossils show dinosaur footprints, nests, or poop.

Many fossils are found far from cities. So, scientists may use helicopters to move fossils.

Scientists bring fossils to **laboratories** to study them. They try to guess what the dinosaurs looked like and how they lived.

STUDYING DINOS

Scientists look at the shapes of dinosaurs' teeth. Teeth can show what dinosaurs ate. Scientists also look at how a dinosaur's bones fit together. That can show how it moved.

Dinosaurs with pointy teeth ate meat. Dinosaurs with flat teeth ate plants.

21

CHAPTER 4

DINOSAUR DISCOVERIES

Scientists use many tools to study fossils. Scans can show what fossils look like inside. And testing nearby rock can help show how old fossils are.

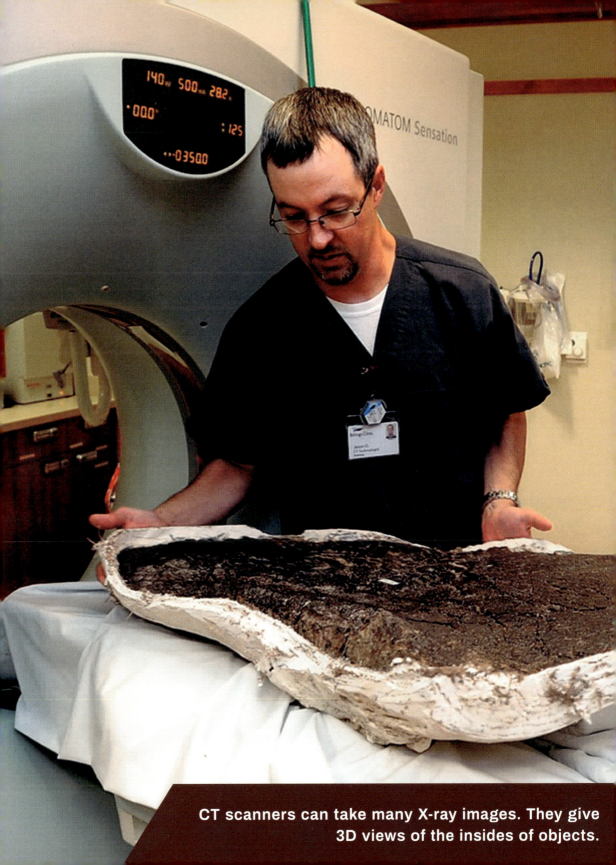

CT scanners can take many X-ray images. They give 3D views of the insides of objects.

Fossils help scientists understand what life was like long ago. They try to learn when each dinosaur **species** lived. This helps them study how Earth changed over time.

FEATHERS

At first, scientists thought dinosaurs were mainly like reptiles. But in the 1990s, fossils showed that many dinosaurs had feathers. In fact, some were the **ancestors** of today's birds.

In 2006, scientists compared feather fossils to modern birds. They learned the color of some dinosaur feathers.

Dinosaurs began living more than 252 million years ago. The last dinosaurs died around 66 million years ago. Scientists think a giant **asteroid** killed them.

Asteroids can be huge. Scientists think the asteroid that killed the dinosaurs was 6 to 9 miles (10 to 15 km) wide.

Some of the oldest dinosaur fossils belong to a group called Herrerasauridae.

FAST FACT
The oldest dinosaur fossil is from 233 million years ago.

COMPREHENSION
QUESTIONS

Write your answers on a separate piece of paper.

1. Write a few sentences explaining the main ideas of Chapter 1.

2. Which type of dinosaur do you like best? Why?

3. When did scientists first use the term *dinosaur*?
   - A. in 1824
   - B. in the early 1840s
   - C. in the 1990s

4. What is one thing scientists could learn by studying dinosaur fossils?
   - A. which types of dinosaurs are not reptiles
   - B. which types of dinosaurs made the most noise
   - C. which types of dinosaurs came before others

5. What does **massive** mean in this book?

*They realized that many kinds of dinosaurs had existed. Some were **massive**. Others were small and quick.*

- **A.** hungry
- **B.** tiny
- **C.** huge

6. What does **fragile** mean in this book?

*Fossils can be **fragile**. So, scientists handle them carefully. They place the fossils in hard cases.*

- **A.** easy to carry
- **B.** easy to break
- **C.** cold and wet

Answer key on page 32.

GLOSSARY

ancestors

Early animals that later animals developed from.

asteroid

A chunk of rock from space that crashed into Earth.

chisels

Metal tools that have blades for cutting, chipping, or carving.

extinct

No longer living on Earth.

fossils

Remains of plants and animals that lived long ago.

laboratories

Places where people study science, often by running tests.

related

Belonging to the same group or family.

sediment

Stone, sand, or other material carried by wind, water, or ice.

species

A group of animals or plants that are similar and can breed with one another.

BOOKS

Allan, John. *Prehistoric Giants*. Lerner Publications, 2025.

Andrews, Elizabeth. *How Birds Evolved*. Abdo Publishing, 2024.

Sabelko, Rebecca. *Allosaurus*. Bellwether Media, 2021.

ONLINE RESOURCES

Visit **www.apexeditions.com** to find links and resources related to this title.

ABOUT THE AUTHOR

Abby Doty is a writer, editor, and booklover from Minnesota.

INDEX

A
ancestors, 24
asteroid, 26

B
Buckland, William, 4, 6–8

C
cases, 18
chisels, 16

E
England, 12

F
fossils, 4, 6, 10, 12, 15, 16, 18–20, 22, 24, 27

L
laboratories, 20
lizards, 6–8, 12

M
Megalosaurus, 8

S
scans, 22
sediment, 15
species, 24

ANSWER KEY:
1. Answers will vary; 2. Answers will vary; 3. B; 4. C; 5. C; 6. B